The Power of Baptism

By Leland Stevens and Jane L. Fryar

CPH

SAINT LOUIS

Edited by Arnold E. Schmidt

Write to Library for the Blind, 1333 South Kirkwood Road, St. Louis, MO 63122-7295 to obtain these materials in braille or in large print.

1 2 3 4 5 6 7 8 9 10   05 04 03 02 01 00 99 98 97 96

Contents

INTRODUCTION

Baptism is the sacrament of initiation, of belonging, and of identity. Baptism tells us who we are and whose we are. When we feel rootless, our Baptism reminds us that we belong to the family of God. When we feel guilty or ashamed, our Baptism reminds us that we have been forgiven and that we wear the robe of Christ's own righteousness. When we feel restless and when we wonder about the meaning of our life, our Baptism reminds us that Christ's call to discipleship rests on our life. We serve the Lord Christ (Colossians 3:23).

God intends that Baptism shape our lives. It's not a long-ago-and-far-away sacrament. It carries power—God's power to save. But how do we plug into this power? How does the sign of the cross that marks our soul impact how we see and respond to events, people, triumphs, and tragedies? And how can we touch our students in such a way that the refrain that marks their lives is: *I am baptized!*

First, we need to immerse ourselves more and more thoroughly in our own baptismal relationship with God so that by His grace we live in the joy, comfort, and power Baptism brings. This book is designed to help you do that. Each chapter ends with some questions designed to apply specific truths in both your own life and in the lives of your students. The appendix adds more practical implications and ideas for integrating baptismal language, symbolism, and truths into the ongoing life you share with your students.

May you see yourself washed from your sins, signed by the cross, robed in Christ's righteousness, and named as God's own in your Baptism as you read and teach.

1

Named by God

Think back to the first time you met with the young people in your class. Do you remember some of your goals for that first day? Probably you worked hard to learn and remember each student's name. Even if you already knew them, you may have incorporated their names into some kind of activity or bulletin board display. You welcomed each individual by name.

Even as adults, most of us feel pleased when others remember our name. Department store managers sometimes encourage their employees to call customers by name as they thank us for our purchases. Perhaps you've experienced the joy of hearing someone else pray for you by name.

What's going on here? Why does our name mean so much to us?

MY NAME, MY SELF

Simply put, your name sums up the total of all that makes you. If you doubt that, name these names out loud:

Abraham Lincoln
Adolf Hitler
Marilyn Monroe
Jesse Jackson
Florence Nightingale

Upon hearing each name, a picture of the person probably flashed across your mind's eye. You probably also thought of that person's words, attitudes, and actions. These people have "made a name for themselves," for better or worse. Not just famous people, but all of us find our names fused with our identity, with who we are and what we have done.

In Baptism, God names us. A baby's Baptism is more than a human ceremony in which parents give their child its legal name. Instead, the name we receive from God in Baptism determines our identity. Actually, it changes our identity—forever.

OLD NAMES, OLD IDENTITIES

If we are to take God's holy work in Baptism seriously, we first need to take human sinfulness seriously. Think back for a moment to the predicament in which the people at the Tower of Babel found themselves. Perhaps you remember their story, especially their goal:

> As men moved eastward, they found a plain in Shinar and settled there. They said to each other, "Come, let's make bricks and bake them thoroughly." They used brick instead of stone, and tar for mortar. Then they said, "Come, let us build ourselves a city, with a tower that reaches to the heavens, so that we may **make a name for ourselves** and not be scattered over the face of the whole earth." (Genesis 11:2–4, emphasis added)

Still today those who live apart from God in Christ chase this same goal—to make a name for themselves. Not just captains of industry or politicians or movie stars fall into this tar pit. By nature, all human beings are curved in on ourselves. We serve ourselves. We seek our own best interests, regardless of the interests of others. Worse still, our actions and attitudes grow out of who we are at the core of our being, a core that is dead at birth and thoroughly decayed.

Apart from Christ, human beings may walk, talk, laugh, cry, eat, and think. They may have fame, power, or wealth. They may cultivate the reputation of party animals. But in reality all these things amount to only so much makeup on a spiritual corpse. No true relationship with God exists or *can* exist. Whether they realize it or not, "all their lives [these people are] … held in slavery by their fear of death" (Hebrews 2:15). This slavery drives them to make a name for themselves in accomplishments, in family relationships, in pleasure, in acquiring more and more trinkets and toys. But the cavity that lies in the center of their hearts can never, ever be filled by these things.

Can this be true? Are we really all that bad? Sadly, yes. The Scriptures paint a bleak picture of the condition of those without Christ. Consider just three of the many New Testament passages that address this issue:

> *The god of this age has **blinded the minds** of unbelievers, so that they **cannot see** the light of the gospel of the glory of Christ, who is the image of God.* (2 Corinthians 4:4, emphasis added)

> *As for you, you were **dead in your transgressions and sins**, in which you used to live when you followed the ways of this world and of the ruler of the kingdom of the air, the spirit who is now at work in those who are disobedient. All of us also lived among them at one time, gratifying the cravings of our sinful nature and following its desires and thoughts. Like the rest, we were **by nature objects of wrath**.* (Ephesians 2:1–3, emphasis added)

> *You were **separate from Christ** … **without hope and without God** and without God in the world.* (Ephesians 2:12, emphasis added)

MORE BAD NEWS

This blindness, death, and separation from the Creator (original sin) causes us to commit all kinds of actual sins. In other words, who we are dictates what we do. Here's one of the apostle Paul's descriptions of the lifestyle of those who live apart from God:

> *They have become filled with every kind of wickedness, evil, greed and depravity. They are full of envy, murder, strife, deceit and malice. They are gossips, slanderers, God-haters, insolent, arrogant and boastful; they invent ways of doing evil; they disobey their parents; they are senseless, faithless, heartless, ruthless. Although they know God's righteous decree that those who do such things deserve death, they not only continue to do these very*

things but also approve of those who practice them. (Romans 1:29–32)

Look at Paul's list again. It's notable, perhaps, for what he does *not* include. No armed robbery. No torture of children. No genocide. Though certainly these sinful actions also grow out of sinful hearts, the apostle focuses on garden-variety, everyday sins: gossip, envy, the lack of love. Even society's most upstanding citizens must plead guilty to sins like these now and again. And with that guilty plea all sinners testify to the condition of their hearts.

Our basic condition is not that we are sinners because we sin occasionally; rather, we commit sins because we are sinners. It's a question of identity, and our identity determines our destiny. And that destiny is not a happy thought:

Those who do such things deserve death. (Romans 1:32)

For the wages of sin is death. (Romans 6:23)

The soul who sins is the one who will die. ... The wickedness of the wicked will be charged against him. (Ezekiel 18:20)

A NEW IDENTITY

The verdict has rung out in heaven's court: GUILTY! The gavel of judgment has fallen. The prisoners have been sentenced to death—you and I among them. If we realize what that means for life today and for our fate at physical death, we can't help but shudder. The sentence of eternal death drives us to run even harder and faster to escape the holy God.

The death warrant cannot be changed. But what if *we* could be changed? What if somehow both our name and our identity were different? What if Sinner could become Saint? The warrant would no longer apply to us. We could slide out from under the fear. We could stop running away from God. We could live without looking over our shoulder, without trying to cover our tracks.

That, the Bible teaches, is precisely what happens in Baptism. Our own attempts to make a name for ourselves prove only how much we need a new name. We cannot manufacture a new identity for ourselves. All the forgers in the world working together into eternity could not produce enough fake I.D. cards to remove the death sentence that hangs over our heads. But our Judge has had compassion on us. He says to you and to me, "Let Me give you a new name."

But how can this be? Is our Judge corrupt? Or some kind of doddering Grandfather in the sky who winks at our offenses? No. Justice had to be served, and indeed has been served, in the person and work of Jesus Christ, the Judge's own Son. We receive the blessings of Baptism, not because Baptism is some kind of magic ritual or legal loophole, but because of what Jesus did for each one of us on His cross:

> *Baptism … now saves you also—not the removal of dirt from the body but the pledge of a good conscience toward God. It saves you by the resurrection of Jesus Christ.* (1 Peter 3:21)

Because Jesus Christ died for our sins and was raised to life again, we receive complete forgiveness of all our sins. We can enjoy a clear conscience. We have a new name, a new identity. God's baptized children are saints, literally His "holy ones." We have been set apart as unique, as belonging to Him, as the sons and daughters of the King. Read what the apostle Peter says about that and note the *then* and *now* of our identity:

> *You are a chosen people, a royal priesthood, a holy nation, a people belonging to God, that you may declare the praises of Him who called you out of darkness into his wonderful light. Once you were not a people, but now you are the people of God; once you had not received mercy, but now you have received mercy.* (1 Peter 2:9–10)

WE HAVE BEEN RENAMED

The words of Baptism itself cut to the heart of our new name. Read your own name in the blank below:

_____, I baptize you in the name of the Father and of the Son and of the Holy Spirit.

A simple formula. But one with life-changing power. We have been named by the name of the Triune God. We belong to Him. We carry the mark of the redeemed, the sign of the cross. We have been adopted into God's family.

That's why our worship services begin with this same Invocation. As the family of God gathers, we remind ourselves that we come as His baptized children. It's why Martin Luther recommended that we make the sign of the cross over ourselves as we come to God in prayer. These are two ways we can remind ourselves often of who we are and whose we are.

WHAT DOES THIS MEAN?

First, our new identity gives us a new destiny. Just think about that destiny summarized for us in Paul's letter to the believers in Colossae: *[We are] giving thanks to the Father, who has qualified you to share in the inheritance of the saints in the kingdom of light. For He has rescued us from the dominion of darkness and brought us into the kingdom of the Son He loves, in whom we have redemption, the forgiveness of sins (Colossians 1:12–14).*

This change of identity changes everything! A change in loyalties. A change in the way we look at our lives and live them. A change from despair to confident hope. A change from condemnation to acquittal in heaven's court. A change from spiritual poverty to the unfathomable riches of God's grace here and now, and the mansions of heaven when we die.

Second, identity influences attitudes and behavior. If our old self—the corrupt, decaying, sinful self—led us into sinful words and actions, then just think about the holy words and actions God has now made possible by giving us a new, holy identity! Recognizing the power of that identity, the apostles over and over in the New Testament appeal to God's people, "Be who you are!" We don't do this because we have to, but because we can. We live as God's children because that's who He has made us to be.

The power of Baptism for daily living: a new identity!

Into the Classroom

1. When have I seen my students respond to the power of a new identity as, perhaps, an athlete, an honor-roll student, the class clown? What evidence does this response give about the power of a person's identity?

2. Since I believe that God has truly given each student in my class a new identity as His dearly loved, holy son or daughter, how will that affect my own relationships with them?

3. How can I communicate more fully to each student in my class the powerful transformation, the change in identity, that God has worked in their hearts through their Baptism?

Do infants need this change of identity too?

The Bible clearly says yes. Take Psalm 51:5, for example: "Surely I was sinful at birth, sinful from the time my mother conceived me." True, infants cannot lie or steal or lust. With them, as with us, the problem lies much deeper than simply outward actions. Like some terrible genetic effect, all of us inherit a spiritually dead heart. We are born "objects of wrath," as Paul puts it in Ephesians 2:3.

Among other things, in Baptism we receive a new relationship with God. We become spiritually alive. This is completely His gift through the work of Jesus on Calvary's cross for us. We do nothing to earn it or to deserve it. A newborn infant adopted into the family of a billionaire will continue to eat and sleep and wet its diapers, but the adoption changes almost everything else in its life. How much greater the change for infants adopted by God into His family and made heirs of the riches of His grace!

2

Washed in the Water

Most human beings find themselves drawn to the spectacular. Flares. Fireworks. The roar of the ocean at high tide. Thunderbolts from the blue.

The crowds who followed Christ during His earthly ministry did so, at least in part, because they wanted to see His next miracle, to witness His spectacular deeds. In *Jesus Christ, Superstar* King Herod urges Jesus, "Walk across my swimming pool." The sentiment behind the command no doubt crossed Herod's mind. (See also Luke 23:8.)

Given human fascination with the sensational, how disappointing Baptism can seem at first blush. How interesting can a handful of water be? Even Baptism by immersion usually involves no more than two or three bathtubs full of water. No ocean roar here. Quite unspectacular. Or is it?

WATER AND THE WORD

If Baptism were water only and nothing else, we could perhaps consider it a let down, a spiritual disappointment. But our Lord has connected His Word to Baptism's waters. And that connection makes all the difference in the world because God's Word carries with it all of God's almighty power.

Slow your reading for a few moments while you picture in your mind's eye God's Word at work. Think of these instances that show the power of that Word:

- Darkness. A darkness thicker than that of any cave in the deepest bowels of the earth. The Lord speaks into that darkness and scatters it forever with a single sentence, "Let there be light." That's the power of the Word as described in Genesis 1. The power of creation.

- A cemetery. Grave upon grave as far as the eye can see. Christ speaks two words, "Come forth," and every grave begins to open. Bodies long ago reduced to dust are restored as each individual soul reunites with its body and the great Judgment Day arrives. That's the power of the Word as described in John 5:28–29. The power of life.

- Early morning in Jerusalem's temple. Jesus sits teaching. The religious leaders throw a prostitute onto the floor at His feet. "We caught her in the act," they sneer. "The law says that we must stone her. To death. What do You say?" At Jesus' rebuke the accusers leave. Then He speaks to the whore. His Word revokes the death sentence and transforms her life. "Neither do I condemn you. Go now and leave your life of sin." That's the power of the Word as described in John 8:1–11. The power of pardon and release.

God speaks. That's how He accomplishes everything He does. He spoke, and the universe leaped into being. He spoke, and Christ Jesus was incarnate and born of the Virgin Mary to suffer and die for our sins. He will speak at the Last Day and the sky will roll up like a scroll bringing history to an end. God does what He does by means of His Word. What power that Word packs!

THE HOLY ORDINARY

In Baptism, God links His Word with ordinary water to accomplish extraordinary things. Not the water, not the amount of water, not the special properties of water do what God wants done. Rather, His promises to us provide the power that make Baptism's water so dynamic.

- The waters of Baptism are a channel through which God pours out His forgiveness of our sins, the forgiveness won by Jesus on the cross. God has cleared us of all charges.

> *And now what are you waiting for? Get up, be baptized and wash your sins away, calling on His name.* (Acts 22:16)

> *Peter replied [to the Pentecost crowd terrorized by their part in crucifying Christ], "Repent and be baptized, every one of you, in the name of Jesus Christ for the forgiveness of your sins."* (Acts 2:38)

- In Baptism God conveys to us the peace of a clear conscience. When Satan attacks and accuses us of greed or selfishness, of a lack of love toward God or others, we can remember that we have been washed clean from the stain of each and every sin. The guilt of that sin that could legitimately rob us of sleep every night of our lives is gone, washed away.

> *This water [the water of Noah's flood] symbolizes baptism that now saves you also—not the removal of dirt from the body but the pledge of a good conscience toward God. It saves you by the resurrection of Jesus Christ.* (1 Peter 3:21)

- In Baptism the Holy Spirit of God comes to indwell us, creating a faith relationship with God and making our hearts His holy temple.

> *Peter replied [to the Pentecost crowd], "Repent and be baptized, every one of you, in the name of Jesus Christ ... and you will receive the gift of the Holy Spirit."* (Acts 2:38)

> *He saved us, not because of righteous things we had done, but because of His mercy. He saved us through the washing of rebirth and renewal by the Holy Spirit.* (Titus 3:5)

PARDON, RECREATION, NEW LIFE

Baptism is not some magical, heavenly hocus pocus. None of the blessings of Baptism come to us apart from the saving work of Christ our Lord. Baptism has the power it has because Jesus has done what He did. And since He has died for our sins and been raised again for our justification, Baptism now does indeed have great power.

In Baptism God's Word accomplishes the very things God has always sent His Word to do. In the waters of Baptism, God declares before all heaven and hell that He has pardoned our sins and released us from their penalty. In the waters of Baptism God creates within us a holy heart, a desire to please Him, a new power to live as His people. In the waters of Baptism God plants within us the seed of eternal life. That life, once begun, will continue into all eternity.

WHAT DOES THIS MEAN?

In "A Mighty Fortress Is Our God" Martin Luther included a stanza about the fury of Satan and the war this enemy wages against Christ and His people. The stanza concludes with this declaration of victory: "One little word can fell him." What is that "word"? Luther identified it as the statement, "I am baptized."

Satan loves to attack God's children with accusations. He enjoys watching us squirm when he infests our hearts with feelings of guilt and shame. When we find ourselves harassed and burdened with a guilty conscience, our Lord invites us to remember what He has done for us in our Baptism:

> But you were washed, you were sanctified, you were justified in the name of the Lord Jesus Christ and by the Spirit of our God. (1 Corinthians 6:11)

The power of Baptism for daily living: freedom from guilt and shame!

Into the Classroom

- What Jesus did for us on Calvary is transmitted to us through Baptism as a means of grace. To show this, turn on a faucet to release water or talk about what happens when a person turns on a faucet. Stress that the faucet doesn't make the water; rather, the water comes from a source—a well, lake, river, or reservoir. So baptism does not "make" forgiveness for us. Christ earned forgiveness for all people by what He did on the cross. Baptism is one channel through which this forgiveness flows to each of us.

- Because God chose to use water in Baptism, we can recall His gifts to us in Baptism many times each day. Whenever you wash your hands or take a drink, remember that you have been washed in the river of His grace and that you can stand before God with a clean conscience. Thank Him for His pardon and peace. Then encourage your students to do the same kind of remembering and thanking.

Must someone be baptized to be saved?

A faith relationship with God through Jesus Christ saves, and that alone. We cannot contribute to our salvation by anything else we do, not even getting baptized. If we think of Baptism as some kind of good work by which we earn God's favor, we change Gospel into Law. Baptism then becomes for us a duty rather than God's gift of grace. God does, of course, command Baptism. But we can rightly think of this command as a command of grace, something like a parent who prepares the family's favorite meal and then invites, "Come to dinner."

The thief on the cross who believed in Jesus received from our Lord's own lips the assurance of life in heaven at the moment of his earthly death. He will be there even though circumstances kept him from being baptized. On the other hand, someone who would refuse Baptism betrays a heart hardened to the grace of God and cynical about His good gifts. It's hard to imagine that saving faith could exist in such a heart. As stated by an early church father, Augustine, it is not the lack of Baptism that condemns, but the refusal to be baptized.

3

Signed by the Cross

Years ago a newspaper story reported the drowning death of a father who had swum out to Australia's Barrier Reef with his son. The father had overestimated his ability to keep up with his son and to swim back to shore. The two rested on the rocks, the tide coming in, with little time left before rocks and father and son would be inundated.

The son pleaded for permission to help his father back to shore as they swam together. But the father knew his son would lose his own life if he attempted such a rescue. Forcefully the father ordered his son to swim to shore alone. Unwilling, but obedient, the son did. The father perished on the rocks; the son made it to shore safely.

This is a gripping story of sacrifice of one human being for another. The father gave up his life for his son. What love! But think for a moment also about the pain in the son's heart as he swam, knowing the sacrifice his father was making at that moment.

A LOVE PERSONAL AND UNIQUE

If you can feel this young man's grief, then perhaps you can begin to imagine how difficult it must have been for God the Father to watch His Son suffer and die for us on the cross. How pain must have ripped through the heavenly Father's heart as Jesus experienced the terrors of hell in our place. How it must have hurt when, instead of comforting, rescuing, and delivering, the Father had to turn His back and leave Jesus to suffer alone. How our Savior's anguish must have shrieked in the Father's ears: "My God, My God, why have You forsaken Me?"

And that is what the heavenly Father did—for us—as He sacrificed His Son to rescue us. We were, at the time, His enemies, held hostage by sin, death, and the devil. Again and again we were dashed against the rocks of our own Barrier Reef—despair, guilt, emptiness. Think of it! "God demonstrates His own love for us in this: While we were still sinners, Christ died for us" (Romans 5:8).

No symbol, no trademark, no logo is as universally well-known as the cross. It stands above all history as a reminder of costly, overwhelming, sacrificial love. And that love is personal. God loved *you* so much that He gave His Son into death for your sins. Each day your life is crossed by God's love, even as your heart and mind were signed by the cross of Christ at your Baptism.

Human minds could not have invented the story of divine love that cut to that depth. Christianity is unique among world religions for its ability to take away the fear and uncertainty regarding our relationship to God. That uniqueness centers in Christ's cross.

A young man reared by Hindu parents tells that he went with his family each day into a Hindu temple to pray. As he looked around inside the temple, he saw the lounging, sitting, sleeping gods to whom the people prayed. The idols, covered with dust, gave no hint whatsoever of concern for the human beings who knelt in worship before them.

Later, after the family's emigration to England, the young man entered a Christian church for the first time. The crucifix on the altar touched him deeply. Later he remarked, "That God should give His Son for me ... that convinced me of His love and of the fact of my hope for the fullest life with Him."

No wonder Christians so treasure the familiar words of John 3:16—"For God so loved the world that He gave His one and only Son, that whoever believes in Him shall not perish but have eternal life."

THE SCANDAL OF THE CROSS (AND OF BAPTISM)

Still, despite the appeal of such love, many down through history and still today reject the cross and the Savior who hung there in our place. Why? Because of sinful blindness. Human beings may totally reject their need for a Savior. Or they may trick themselves into believing they have something to offer God in exchange for His love. They buy Satan's lie that God can't possibly be as generous as He says He is. They look for the strings attached to the Good News, and they try to create loopholes through which they can insert their own goodness. Surely there must be something they can do to prove that they deserve God's compassion. Or, perhaps, something they can do to pay Him back for His free gifts.

The truth is that we cannot earn God's love or repay Him for that love. The cross stands, a silent rebuke to those who cling to the false hope of human merit. The scandal of the cross. Paul wrote about it in these words:

> We preach Christ crucified: a stumbling block [or scandal] to Jews and foolishness to Gentiles, but to those whom God has called, both Jews and Greeks, Christ the power of God and the wisdom   of   God.
> (1 Corinthians 1:23)

Baptism presents exactly the same scandal. We do nothing and we *can* do nothing to earn or deserve the blessings God gives here. These blessings are in fact the blessings Christ earned for us on His cross. In Baptism, God personalizes them. He wraps them up in a single package, ties it with a bow, and attaches a tag with our own name inscribed on it. *From God to You. With Love.*

We simply receive. Baptism is pure Gospel, pure gift. The power of God and the wisdom of God. But this power and wisdom scandalize those who insist on trying to turn the Gospel into a "To Do List" of human works.

23

CRUCIFIED, BURIED, AND RAISED WITH CHRIST

The cross. Our hearts burn when we think of all Christ accomplished there for us. You undoubtedly understand the power of Christ's cross to assure you of forgiveness of sins and eternal life. But do you realize the incredible power of that cross at work *through your Baptism* to give you victory over the pull of sin in your life right now? Or, to put it another way, have you ever longed to get out from under the wrong thoughts, attitudes, words, and actions that seem to hold you hostage? You need look no further than the baptismal font and the connection the Holy Spirit forged there between you and the Lord Christ.

Listen to the way Paul describes that link in Romans 6:3–4:

> *Don't you know that all of us who were baptized into Christ Jesus were baptized into His death? We were therefore buried with Him through baptism into death in order that, just as Christ was raised from the dead through the glory of the Father, we too may live a new life.*

In a way that no human being can fully understand, your old self and mine hung on Christ's cross with Him. Through Baptism our natural, sinful nature died on Calvary with Christ. And now we have also been raised with Christ to live a brand new life. This is *not* just symbolic or some flowery way to describe a philosophical ideal. It is unquestionably true.

Yes, our union with Christ in His death and resurrection is a mystery. It might be more accurate to describe it as mystical, for Paul uses mystical language. But the more the Holy Spirit enlightens our hearts so that we see this tremendous truth with more and more clarity, the more power it exerts in our lives.

NEW LIFE AND FREEDOM TO LIVE IT

The Middle Ages saw the invention of many terrible forms of torture and execution. In one of the most ghastly, a prisoner condemned to death was shackled face to face to a corpse and then locked in a cell alone until death mercifully came. Who can imagine the horror, the misery, the terror that the condemned person surely experienced? Insanity must have come within a few hours in most cases.

In some ways, your life before Baptism was like that. Shackled to your old nature, you endured a living death. Dead and decaying, your sinful nature pulled you relentlessly toward the grave and the hell that lay beyond it. Not only that, Satan himself served as your jailer. He held the keys to your cell.

But in Baptism, that living death sentence ended. The execution order that stood against you was carried out as you died with Christ. And when Christ rose from death, you arose too! The shackles that held you captive to your old nature fell off.

Now you are no longer obligated to follow that old nature around. You need no longer do what it wants you to do. When you were tied to it, you had no choice. In fact, you wanted no other choice. But the torture of that kind of life has ended—forever! Christ's resurrection, at work in you through your Baptism, has released the shackles. Not only that, your Savior has snatched the keys of hell and death from Satan and opened your prison door (Revelation 1:18).

You are free! What incredible relief! And what incredible power comes with that freedom. It's real power—power we need daily, for our old nature did not simply give up when it saw what Christ had done for us. It didn't lie down and expire. No, instead it teamed up with its old ally, Satan. The two had been in partnership all along anyway, so their alliance now should come as no surprise.

They follow us around, hounding us with their lies. They want to convince us that we belong back in the prison of guilt. They want us to believe that we still must follow the pattern of living death they have in mind for us. They want to suck us back into the selfish, loveless, lonely lifestyle that kept us from the joy and peace that God has wanted for us all along.

That unholy alliance prompts Paul to explain in detail the power of Baptism for holy living in Romans 6:1–14. After he outlines the truth about our death, burial, and resurrection with Christ, he says, "In the same way, count yourselves dead to sin but alive to God in Christ Jesus" (6:11). In other words, think of yourselves in this new way. You are *not* in bondage anymore. You live Christ's new life. In fact, He lives His new life in You! In Him you have the power that enables you not to let Satan and your old nature trick you back into slavery.

WEAPONS OF RIGHTEOUSNESS

From ancient times, the rite of Baptism has included this question and response:

> *Q: Do you renounce the devil and all his works and all his ways?*

> *A: I do renounce them.*

This question and its answer are not some quaint formality. In Baptism a person changes sides in the cosmic war between good and evil. Our loyalties switch. We, who had by nature sworn allegiance to Satan and his forces, from now on belong to the living, Triune God and serve His kingdom. In Baptism we desert the forces of darkness as God transfers us to the kingdom of light (Colossians 1:13). The battle does not ease at that point; rather, it intensifies. Listen to Paul in Romans 6 again:

> *Do not offer the parts of your body to sin, as instruments of wickedness, but rather offer yourselves to God, as those who have been brought from death to life; and offer the parts of your body to Him as instruments of righteousness.* (6:13)

We are at war. The apostle here acknowledges that the battle we fight with sin, Satan, and with our old nature is a real battle. But (and this is the encouraging part) victory is now possible, and not only possible but assured. Paul follows these instructions with a promise. As you read it, note that it truly *is* a promise, not a command:

> *For sin shall not be your master, because you are not under law, but under grace.* (6:14)

Will we still sin after Baptism? Unfortunately, yes. The pull of sin and Satan will still be there. But our slipups need not lead to despair. We are not yet what we will be when Christ returns to take us to Himself in heaven. But, thank God, we are no longer what we were. We are no longer slaves to our old nature and prisoners of Satan. We are forgiven. We are free. And we have the power to use our freedom to bring glory to God and to share His joy, love, and peace with others.

When temptations cross our minds, we can remember who we are—Christ's baptized people. We can focus on the new life we have through our death and resurrection with Christ. We can appeal to our Lord for His protection and strength. We can ask our brothers and sisters in the faith for encouragement and help. And we can hide in our Lord's deep love for us until the storm of the temptation passes.

The power of Baptism for daily living: a new freedom from slavery to sin and Satan!

Into the Classroom

1. In years gone by, Christians often had their baptismal certificates framed and hung on their bedroom wall. Each night, before they went to sleep, it reminded them of who they were—Christ's forgiven people. Each morning when they awoke, it reminded them of who they were—Christ's empowered people. What could you do to remind yourself, each day, of who you now are in Christ and His cross? What kind of craft or other project could your students make to serve the same purpose?

2. Do you ever use the sign of the cross in your personal or public worship life? How could doing so before your devotions or after the Lord's Supper remind you of the power Christ gives you through your Baptism? Might you want to teach your students something about this practice and the reasons behind it? Explain.

3. Which of the truths from Romans 6:1–14 would you like to incorporate more fully into your own view of yourself and your Lord's work for you? Which of these truths would be helpful to the children or young people you teach? Talk with your pastor and with other teachers in

your congregation and pray together about what you could do to facilitate this new learning.

How should water be applied?

Some churches teach that for Baptism to be valid, one must be immersed. But the word baptize means to apply water by immersing, washing, pouring, and the like. Therefore some Christians usually just sprinkle or pour a small amount of water on the person's head.

In the imagery of Romans 6 Baptism involves dying, being buried, and rising with Christ. Baptism by immersion certainly illustrates in a powerful way the blessings that God conveys to us through Baptism. Furthermore, immersion was probably the most common form for Baptism in the early church, and it continues to be the prevailing practice in the Eastern Church to this day, including the immersion of babies. Even so, very early documents describing the practice of the early church refer to Baptisms in which water was simply poured on the candidate in place of immersion.

Historical precedent aside, we might answer the question "How much water?" by asking another question "Where does Baptism receive its power?" If it comes from the water, then perhaps the more water the better. But if it comes from the Word of God connected to the water (as it does), then the amount of water matters little. As we saw in chapter 2, Baptism by immersion gives to the baptized person all the blessings of Christ, because God connects His Word of promise to the water. Baptism by pouring or sprinkling communicates those same blessings for exactly the same reason.

4

Robed in Christ's Righteousness

Henry David Thoreau once gave this advice: "Beware of all enterprises that require new clothes." He was no doubt thinking of the way human beings sometimes substitute appearance for reality. And people do often try to cover up uncertainty or incompetence by dressing as if they were certain or competent. On the other hand, when we know we look our best, it often gives us the confidence to do our best. That's one reason why athletic teams buy striking uniforms and public speakers seldom dress in blue jeans or tattered flannel shirts.

The New Testament comes back again and again to the idea that when we were baptized, God clothed us with the robe of Christ's righteousness. Over and over the apostle Paul reminds his readers that we are now "in Christ." These two ideas are tied together so closely that we can't separate them.

CLOTHED WITH CHRIST

Most children learn the story about the Emperor's New Clothes. Not satisfied by either his riches or power, the emperor hires some crafty tailors who promise to make for him clothing so enchanted that fools will not be able to see it. They pretend to work for weeks, stashing away the gold that the emperor gladly pays them for producing such marvelous clothing. When the emperor wears the clothing for the first time, all his subjects oooh and aahh over it. They do not want to be thought of as fools. Finally a boy too young to know better points out the obvious: The emperor stands before his people stark naked.

Despite the truth embedded in the fable, the world system around us still tries to sell us "new clothes." People down through history have, for the most part, rejected their need for Christ's robe of righteousness. Instead, they have opted to cover up their inadequacy with the three "P's"—possessions, power, prestige.

Sometimes even we as believing, baptized Christians reach deep into the closet of our hearts and select one of these outfits to cover up our insecurity. Like little children, we let ourselves be fooled into believing that more toys will make us happy; or that "being boss" will satisfy our need to belong; or that if "the other kids" like us, we will learn to like ourselves. Can it be that those things will leave us just as naked as the emperor, spiritually speaking? You know the answer to that—a resounding yes!

That's why it's so good to know that we need not settle for the tattered rags of that kind of spiritual clothing. Listen as the apostle Paul compares the rags the world offers us with the right standing before God that comes from being clothed in Christ:

> I consider everything a loss compared to the surpassing greatness of knowing Christ Jesus my Lord, for whose sake I have lost all things. I consider them rubbish, that I may gain Christ and be found in Him, not having a righteousness of my own that comes from the law, but that which is through faith in Christ— the righteousness that comes from God and is by faith. (Philippians 3:8–9, emphasis added)

But how can we be sure we have that kind of clothing? How do we know that we are "in Christ" and that we wear the robe of His righteousness? Again, the apostle Paul answers the question:

> All of you who were baptized into Christ have clothed yourselves with Christ. (Galatians 3:27)

ONCE AND FOREVER

Christ's robe of righteousness differs from our everyday clothing. We dress and undress each day, often more than once. But when we put on Christ's righteousness, that garment is ours forever. Wearing it, God empowers us to respond to other people and to the challenges of life in much the same way as Christ Himself would. His robe of righteousness shapes our behavior.

When an athlete is in uniform and knows it, it alters the way she walks and talks. Sometimes a little. Sometimes a lot. If she belongs to a winning team, she may show more confidence both on and off the field. She may wave to fans whom ordinarily she wouldn't even acknowledge. She may unconsciously react with more assertiveness if she's cut off in traffic or if she feels she's being treated unfairly by a surly clerk.

When a soldier is in uniform and knows it, it alters the way he walks and talks. Sometimes a little. Sometimes a lot. He will stand at attention during the national anthem. He will salute his superiors, even sometimes when they themselves are out of uniform. He may carry himself a bit straighter. He may unconsciously call even the most impolite clerks "sir" or "ma'am."

In a similar way, when we as Christ's people wear His robe of righteousness and realize it, it alters the way we live. That robe is our "uniform," if you will. It marks us as belonging to Him and to one another. And in a way no earthly uniform could, it conveys to us the power to live like the people it says we are. Paul summed up that lifestyle and the power behind it in these words:

> You were taught, with regard to your former way of life, to **put off** your old self, which is being corrupted by its deceitful desires; to **be made new** in the attitude of your minds; and to **put on the new self**, created to be like God in true righteousness and holiness.

> Therefore each of you must put off falsehood and speak truthfully to his neighbor, for we are all members of one body. "In your anger do not sin": Do not let the sun go down while you are still angry, and do not give the devil a foothold.

33

He who has been stealing must steal no longer, but must work, doing something useful with his own hands, that he may have something to share with those in need.

Do not let any unwholesome talk come out of your mouths, but only what is helpful for building others up according to their needs, that it may benefit those who listen. And do not grieve the Holy Spirit of God, with whom you were sealed for the day of redemption. Get rid of all bitterness, rage and anger, brawling and slander, along with every form of malice.

Be kind and compassionate to one another, forgiving each other, just as in Christ God forgave you.

Be imitators of God, therefore, as dearly loved children and live a life of love, just as Christ loved us and gave himself up for us as a fragrant offering and sacrifice to God.

But among you there must not be even a hint of sexual immorality, or of any kind of impurity, or of greed, because these are improper for God's holy people. Nor should there be obscenity, foolish talk or coarse joking, which are out of place, but rather thanksgiving. (Ephesians 4:22–5:4)

What a lifestyle! "But wait a minute," you may be saying if you read carefully. "This robe of righteousness doesn't sound permanent. It sounds like we have to keep on putting it on, over and over again, just like you'd put on your shirt in the morning."

But look again. In the first paragraph (verses 22–24) of the passage, Paul is simply reminding his readers of what they had been taught. He assumes that their new clothing has already arrived, that they are already in the faith, baptized and thus clothed with Christ. Since this is already true and will continue to be true, then the power to live the lifestyle he commends also belongs to them. **Because they are already clothed with Christ, because they are already "created to be like God in true righteousness and holiness," now they can act like it.** They need not "try hard" to summon up the power inside themselves to live holy lives. They can relax and be who they already are—in Christ and through Baptism.

BEING WHO WE ARE

If this sounds to you like we're back to the new identity we discussed in chapter 1, you're right. To say that each of us has received from Christ His robe of righteousness is simply another way of saying that we have been recreated, made new by faith in Him. This newness comes because of Christ's cross. And it comes through our Baptism.

Paul writes, "If anyone is in Christ, he is a new creation; the old has gone, the new has come!" (2 Corinthians 5:17). The "in Christ" language is, as we have seen, the language of Baptism. We commonly use the word "new" in the familiar sense of new in time or use. So we purchase a new car, or new clothes, or new appliances, or a new home. We get a new position or a new job. Or we wish one another a "Happy New Year."

But the Greek of the New Testament has two different words for "new." One of these means new in the sense we commonly use it. But the other word means *new in point of quality*. This kind of "new" describes *something that has never existed before*. In Christ, we are new in that overwhelming sense: He gives us a quality of life that has never existed before. He gives us new hope. He puts a new song on our lips. He gives us a new outlook, a new purpose, new motivation, new direction. He gives us new joy, new strength, new peace.

To symbolize all this, converts in the early Christian church were baptized without clothing. Men and women, of course, were baptized separately. Deaconesses baptized the women while the pastor or bishop stood behind a screen and spoke the words. When the newly baptized person came up out of the water, he or she was given a new, white robe to signify the robe of righteousness that now belonged to that person in Christ. Hints of this practice can still be seen today in the custom of clothing infants in white for the baptismal service.

Christ's own righteousness is now ours. We have been made new. What a thought! Can you begin to see how different our daily living would be if we would embrace these facts more fully? Can you understand how Christ's robe of righteousness could shape our behaviors and attitudes? Can you envision the possibilities of a life lived conscious of the holiness and beauty that clothes us because we are in Christ?

How the toys and trinkets of possessions, the perks of power, and the facade of power all pale in the light of the beauty that belongs to us who have been baptized into Christ's death and raised with Christ to sit with Him in the heavenly places (Ephesians 2:6–7)!

THE COMMUNITY OF THE BAPTIZED

One last implication of this robe of righteousness you and I wear: all of our brothers and sisters in the faith wear it too. It's a kind of "team jacket," if you will. It links us to Christ and through Christ to one another. Notice the context of a passage we read earlier in this chapter:

"You are all sons of God through faith in Christ Jesus," Paul says, "for all of you who were baptized into Christ have clothed yourselves with Christ." (Galatians 3:26–27, emphasis added)

Once we are "in Christ," we share a common unity, as the very next verse points out:

There is neither Jew nor Greek, slave nor free, male nor female, for you are all one in Christ Jesus. (Galatians 3:28, emphasis added)

Earthly status ceases in God's kingdom. We are all equal— redeemed children of God. By the power of the Holy Spirit we grow in our ability to see other believers as our brothers and sisters in the faith. We become more able to forgive them as we have been forgiven, to show them the same mercy God has shown us, and to walk the aisle of history toward heaven together.

Beneath the cross, we are united with Christ. The differences that, in the world, cause division, lose their power to divide us. Because of our Baptism, we are freed to "love one another deeply, from the heart," having "sincere love for [our] brothers [and sisters]" in the faith (1 Peter 1:22).

The power of Baptism for daily living: a new and right standing before God and a new ability to love others.

Into the Classroom

1. What word pictures from this chapter did you find the most helpful as you thought through this facet of Baptism's blessings? Which word pictures do you think would mean most to your students as they wrestle with the meaning of Baptism for their own lives?

2. How fully do the members of your class live out the fact that they all belong to the "community of the baptized"? How could you facilitate more meaningful community life among your group?

3. If your students were to design a "team jacket" based on the truths in this chapter, what would it look like?

Might a person need to be rebaptized?

If a person walks away from the baptized community, the church, for awhile—months or years, that person does not need to be rebaptized when he or she returns. If you're already wearing your coat, it's impossible to put it on again. It can't be done. If a child has been adopted into a new family, he or she can't be adopted again by the same family. It's a legal impossibility.

In the same way, once God "adopts" a person into His family and seals that adoption in Baptism, the adoption cannot be repeated. It's a legal reality that does not change. Outward behavior does not void the adoption or forfeit the robe of righteousness. Remember, the status God confers upon His baptized people comes to us as His gift, and does not depend in any way on what we do.

Of course, any number of people each year appear on the doorsteps of churches and go through the motions of Baptism for the second (or third or fourth) time. But nothing changes in heaven's hall of records. Blessings have never been revoked, so they cannot be reconferred.

5

Shine Out!

Every time we witness a Baptism in our church, we are reminded that it is God who names us. We hear again those beautiful, familiar words, "I baptize you in the name of the Father and of the Son and of the Holy Spirit."

As we watch the pastor make the sign of the cross on the person's forehead and chest, we realize again that the cross crosses every event of our lives from the time of our own Baptism to that day when we meet our Lord face to face in the glories of heaven.

As we watch someone be washed in the waters of Baptism, we remember God's covenant promise to forgive us. Our own Baptism assures us that each time we come before God to confess our sins, we can know for sure that those sins are indeed drowned and our pardon is certain.

When a baby is baptized, its white dress symbolizes for us the robe of Christ's righteousness that all God's believing, baptized children wear. And we can sing within ourselves the familiar words:

> Nothing in my hand I bring;
> Simply to Your cross I cling.
> Naked, come to You for dress;
> Helpless, look to You for grace;
> Foul, I to the fountain fly;
> Wash me, Savior, or I die.

Just before the baptismal liturgy ends, pastor and people approach the altar. The congregation prays on behalf of the newly baptized. Then, in many churches, a baptismal candle is lighted from either the paschal or altar candle and presented to the baptized person with these instructions:

> *Receive this burning light. Live always by the light of Christ, and be ever watchful for His coming that you may meet Him with joy and enter with Him to the marriage feast of the Lamb in His kingdom, which shall have no end.*

These words echo the words of our Lord Jesus in Matthew 5:16—"Let your light shine before men, that they may see your good deeds and praise your Father in heaven."

Though the rite has ended, the power remains. And the baptized person begins the lifelong privilege of walking in that power, in the light of God's grace.

LIGHT FOR DARKNESS

"Let your light shine," Jesus says to us each day of our lives. In these words He holds out to us the certainty of our new identity. He Himself makes it possible for us to be lights in the darkness of this world's sin. With His cross, He has bridged the chasm of the sins that used to lie between us and our heavenly Father. In Christ, our sins separate us no longer from our Father's embrace. We can be absolutely certain that God loves and forgives us. We have been made new creations.

Now we are to light up the darkness of our world. But like a single candle shining out into the darkness of a midnight prairie, we may question what kind of difference we can possibly make. Given the billions of people on earth and the complexity of today's social problems, we may feel the temptation to despair, to give up. When that happens, God would have us once again remember our Baptism. He would have us think carefully about the thrill of His promise that we will be light to the world, because He has made us so.

How effective one candle of light can be!

- When one Christian shows Christ's strong, forgiving love again and again, she is a light to the world.

- When one Christian stands up to wrongdoing and rejects society's rationalizations excusing it, he is a light to the world.

- When one Christian controls selfish desires and wants and pours herself out in service for others, she is a light to the world.

- When one Christian speaks up in love to witness to Jesus and the message of compassion and forgiveness He brings to hurting, lonely, guilty people, especially then, he is a light to the world.

When we penetrate the world's darkness by giving ourselves even in small ways so that others may see Jesus and His way more clearly, we are light in the world's darkness. We may not always realize it. In fact, it's better for us to be so caught up in Christ-confident, self-forgetful love that we have little time to take readings with any kind of spiritual light meter to see how we're doing.

Remember Moses? After he had spent 40 days on the mountain with God, his face shone from the glory he had seen. Moses so reflected that glory that it frightened the people of Israel. They didn't know what had happened to him. At first, Moses himself didn't realize what had happened either. The people around him had to tell him about the glory he reflected! Then he veiled his face in response to his people's fears (Exodus 34:29–35).

That's how God wants it to be with us too. As we spend time in His presence reading His Word, at the Holy Table, and in worship, we will receive from Him the fullness of His grace. That grace will transform us. We will become more and more like Jesus. Then others will see His goodness and love radiating from our lives.

But always, our focus needs to rest on Christ: on Christ crucified, on Christ risen and living for us and in us.

SAINT AND SINNER

All this sounds so wonderful. Maybe a bit too wonderful. We know that Baptism doesn't inoculate us against sinning. Even Adolf Hitler was baptized as an infant! An extreme example, to be sure. But a fact we need to explore. How on earth—and in heaven—did it happen? And what does it mean for us?

Along with the sin-darkened nature of the human heart, some early century Christians held a faulty view of Baptism's power to convey God's forgiveness only of sins committed before Baptism. This led them to postpone Baptism as long as possible. The ideal for these people was Baptism on one's death bed! They saw it as an irrevocable ticket to heaven. Of course, the benefits had to be weighed against the dangers of dying an accidental death without the benefit of Baptism at all.

Their view of Baptism was, of course, a kind of magical view. Nonetheless, Baptism does have mighty power to convey God's pardon. We've seen that again and again from the Scriptures as we've discussed the benefits of Baptism in the early chapters of this book. Those in the early church who postponed receiving it failed to understand the *ongoing* power of Baptism for living a holy life.

When the inner person is made righteous by Christ, the character of that person cannot help but glow with Christ's righteousness. On the other hand, while we live on this earth, we will deal with our own weakness and inclination to disobey God. We sometimes do give in to sin and thus cloud the righteousness of Christ that He so generously gave to us in our Baptism. We are, in Luther's classic words, "saint and sinner at the same time."

A BAPTIZED SINNER

We are saints who sin; we are God's holy, righteous people who struggle with the old nature, the sin nature. That's the truth. We see it in Scripture and we observe it each day in our own experience. The critical question is not "Do baptized saints sin?"

Rather, the question we need to ask is **"What do baptized saints do about their sins?"**

First, we recognize them. Our culture reserves the word *sin* to denote things such as serial murder and heinous hate crimes. As God's people, though, we know that sin includes any thought, word, or action by which we disobey God's holy law. In doing so we hurt Him, ourselves, or other people. We recognize our root sin: lovelessness. We see the tendency of our hearts to be so self-absorbed that those around us fail to see in us the light of Christ that should be shining from us.

Second, we confess them. To *confess* in its most basic form means to agree with God, with His Word, and with the convicting power of the Holy Spirit. When we confess our sins, we admit that we have sinned. We not only agree in general with the notion that we are sinners, but we recognize the specific sins of which we are aware. We give up the notion of trying to shift blame onto the shoulders of others. We forego the adult versions of our childhood excuses: *He did it too. She did it first. They did it more. Someone made me. What's so bad about it?* Instead, we simply admit our guilt: *I did it. It was wrong. I deserve to be punished. I need forgiveness.*

Third, we receive God's pardon for Jesus' sake. Remembering the right-standing ("righteousness") our Lord Jesus earned for us on Calvary's cross, we receive God's forgiveness. (Forgiveness—what a beautiful word!) We trust that our guilt has been washed away. Our debt has been paid in full. We cling to God's promise that Christ took our punishment in our place.

Finally, we use the power of Baptism to turn from wrongdoing. God's pardon carries with it His power to live the new lives we received in Baptism. In a way that the world cannot understand, each day is, for a baptized believer, a new day. Remember, "If anyone is in Christ, he is a new creation; the old has gone, the new has come!" (2 Corinthians 5:17). Forgiven, we are truly Christ's holy people empowered to live holy lives. We have from God what it takes to let our light shine for Him.

ECHOES FROM THE PAST

The early Christian church caught fire as her members caught and lived the Gospel message. Other people, still outside the faith, sat up and took notice. They reported that Christ's people had "turned the world upside down" (Acts 17:6).

Cyprian, one of the early church fathers, came to faith and was baptized as an adult. On fire with the love of Christ, he wrote to his friend, Donatus, who was still outside the Christian family:

> This seems a cheerful world, Donatus, when I view it from this fair garden under the shadow of these vines. But if I climbed some great mountain and looked out over the wide lands you know very well what I would see. Brigands on the high roads, pirates on the seas, in the amphitheaters men murdered to please applauding crowds, under all roofs misery and selfishness. It is really a bad world, Donatus, an incredibly bad world. Yet in the midst of it I have found a quiet and holy people. They have discovered a joy which is a thousand times better than any pleasure of this sinful life. They are despised and persecuted but they care not. They have overcome the world. These people, Donatus, are the Christians—and I am one of them.

The power of Baptism for daily living: the ability to live lives radiant with Christ's love!

Into the Classroom

1. Does your congregation use a baptismal candle in any way? If so, is the symbolism explained? What could your class do to help the members of your congregation better understand the imagery of light and Jesus' words to His followers, "You are the light of the world"?

2. If you teach older children, read Cyprian's letter to your group. Does his description of the world as "really a bad world, …, an incredibly bad world" ring true? Why or why not? Do class members see the Christians around them shining with Christ's love in the ways Cyprian describes? Explain. If other people looked at the lives

lived by the members of your class, would they see the light Cyprian saw in the believers around him? Again, ask for evidence to support the opinions students express.

3. Find out whether or not any children, baptized in your congregation the same year as your class, have dropped out of Sunday school, VBS, and public worship. Why has that happened? What could you or the members of your class do to welcome them back? Would it take a personal invitation? a home visit? weekly transportation by a congregational member? or …? Talk with your pastor or the head elder or deacon in your congregation about this.

Will every baptized person go to heaven?

The idea "once baptized, forever saved," has no support whatsoever in Scripture, and it has caused untold damage by creating false security in countless hearts. On the one hand, God does mark us as His own in Baptism. He is zealous to protect and strengthen the faith-relationship He has established with us. No one can snatch us out of His hand (John 10:28). We need not fear sin, hell, Satan, or death. The heavenly Father does not give His children away!

On the other hand, Baptism is not some kind of magical, eternal life insurance policy. If over a period of months or years we resist and resist and resist the Holy Spirit, if we walk away from God and ignore His repeated calls to repentance, if we deliberately give back the robe of righteousness that was ours in Christ—such actions will eventually destroy the relationship God established with us in Baptism. God never breaks His covenant with us, but we can walk out from under the blessings of that covenant relationship.

Even if we do, our Lord will take great pains to come after us, to bring us to repentance. But He will not force anyone to take His gift of salvation in Christ. With continued resistance one finally revokes the blessings God wants so much for us to have and keep.

6

Using Baptism's Power in the Classroom

Bradley stalled around until everyone else had left my seventh grade Sunday school classroom. He fumbled with his leaflet, folding it and sticking it into his Bible. He straightened the classroom Bibles on their rack. When all the other kids were finally out the door, he came to the front of the room where I sat. "My mom won't let me get baptized," he began.

We had studied Israel's crossing the Red Sea that morning. I had drawn comparisons from that account to Baptism. That had led to a discussion of the many times down through history when God has saved His people through water—Noah, baby Moses, ancient Israel, and we ourselves, God's baptized children. I wasn't as precise with my language as I had needed to be.

Bradley had come to our congregation through VBS. A sixth grader at the time, he had been led by the Spirit to a living faith. And, after VBS concluded, he began coming to Sunday school each week. His parents had never darkened the door, but since the family lived within walking distance of the church and since they didn't mind his leaving the house early on Sunday morning, their disinterest had not proven a stumbling block. Until now.

Practicing damage control, I explained more fully to Bradley the fact that faith in Christ Jesus alone saves us. I clarified the power of the Holy Spirit to create faith and the different means by which He chooses to do that. I assured Bradley of

Jesus' eternal love for him and of the total forgiveness that came to him personally through Jesus' cross. And I volunteered to visit his home to talk with his parents. Evidently Bradley had already approached them about Baptism and had met with a negative response.

A few days later, my pastor and I rang Bradley's front doorbell. Dad answered. Mom was at work. We had a cordial conversation. Still, the possibility of Baptism for Bradley was a case closed. Dad didn't care, but Mom would not tolerate the possibility. In fact, Dad warned in a matter-of-fact tone that if we were still in the house when she came home, we'd likely find ourselves sailing over the front railing.

Despite several follow-up phone calls and one or two (courageous!) visits by the pastor, Bradley's parents never budged. I wrestled with the possibility of baptizing him myself. But I couldn't reconcile the blessings and power of the Sacrament with the fact that in order to baptize Bradley I'd have to encourage him to scorn his parents' clear commands. Was this truly a case of "obeying God rather than Mom"? And what might happen to his parents' tolerance of church and Sunday school attendance if they found out the adults at church had encouraged him to disobey them?

After his year in my class, Bradley continued to attend worship services regularly. Eventually, he joined the congregation's youth group. I moved to another city soon thereafter and lost track of him. Still, I think of Bradley at times, and I pray for him. I wonder what happened to his zeal for the Lord, and I envy the people who eventually did get to witness his Baptism. (No, I don't *know* he was eventually baptized, but I trust the Spirit's faithfulness to His call on Bradley's life.)

I learned a lot from Bradley. Not the least of which was the need to choose my words with care when I taught about Baptism to a group that could include unbaptized children or adults.

TIE BAPTISM TO THE CROSS

Without thinking, we can easily misstate what God teaches about Baptism. We can, without intending to, make it seem to children that the act of Baptism saves us, apart from any action by God. As we have seen throughout this book, the Scriptures teach that Baptism is a means or channel of God's grace. Just as the pipes and faucet don't create water, but only deliver it, so also Baptism conveys to us God's blessings, the blessings our Lord Jesus won for us on Calvary's cross. Remember the words of the apostle Peter:

> [The water of Noah's flood] symbolizes baptism that now saves you also—not the removal of dirt from the body but the pledge of a good conscience toward God. **It saves you by the resurrection of Jesus Christ.** (1 Peter 3:21, emphasis added)

To believe or teach anything else changes Baptism into either a magic potion or a "good work" by which we go through some motions that force God to deliver His blessings to us. The blessings of Baptism are tied so tightly to the cross and to Christ's open tomb that if the cord linking them is cut, the power of Baptism is destroyed.

Indeed, God does save infants through Baptism. But He does that by planting in their hearts the seed of faith in the crucified and risen Savior. Such faith is not a thing of the intellect, for no human being can understand God's grace. It is, rather, a relationship.

Think of it this way. An infant, adopted into a loving family, may very well sleep through the court proceedings that validate the adoption. Nonetheless, the adoption creates a whole new life for such a child and gives him or her a whole new family. God adopts infants in Baptism. In a much deeper, spiritual sense He gives them a whole new life, eternal life, in place of the spiritual death that would have condemned them to live cut off from Him forever.

But suppose the same family wanted to adopt an older child. Undoubtedly that child would spend time with the family. He or she would experience the love of Mom and Dad. The child would attend the adoption proceedings with the parents and would likely be asked to talk to the judge about the adoption. Such testimony might go something like this: "These people love me. I want to spend my life as their son/daughter. I belong in this family. Please let me be adopted."

That's somewhat of an analogy to what happens when the church baptizes adults and children old enough to receive instruction. Such individuals learn to know the Savior and His love through His Word. They are nurtured in their new faith by caring brothers and sisters in the faith. Once they understand what God promises to do for them in and through Baptism, they want it for themselves. Their testimony might go something like this: "My Savior loves me. He died for me. He wants me to spend my life as a son/daughter of the heavenly Father. Please let me be baptized."

As we teach about Baptism, especially as we teach groups of children in which some are baptized and some are not, we need to keep Jesus' words in mind: "Whoever believes and is baptized will be saved, but whoever does not believe will be condemned" (Mark 16:16). Based in part on this passage, Augustine concluded, "It is not the lack of Baptism which condemns, but the refusal to be baptized."

ONGOING EFFECTS

When we teach about Baptism, we can gut its power by failing to continually link it to the cross. We can also do that by treating it as an isolated, one-time event rather than as an eternal covenant that has very real effects in the present.

Many Sunday schools, day schools, and midweek schools celebrate baptismal birthdays. Sometimes these celebrations include a song or a candle-lighting ceremony. Often they include a prayer and a small gift. A practice like this can remind children of their Baptism and of at least part of what God has done for them in Baptism.

Still, we need to find ways to help our students understand in a deeper way that "remembering our Baptism" does not simply mean commemorating that day in the dim past when God acted. We need to look for ways to help them see Baptism's power for everyday living. Here are a few suggestions. Perhaps you and the other teachers on your church staff can think of more.

1. In addition to the baptismal birthday celebration at church, the child's teacher or the pastor could send each child a brief note through the mail during the week before or after the celebration. The note could personalize Baptism's meaning for the child in age-appropriate language.

2. In the baptismal service, baptismal sponsors promise to pray for their godchildren. Why not have your students write down prayer-requests and send them to their sponsors? These requests could include the spiritual needs the children feel. (E.g., "The other kids all hate Johnny Sweatshirt, but I know Jesus wants me to be his friend. Pray that I know how to do that." "I'm starting confirmation this year and I have a hard time memorizing all these passages. Pray that the Holy Spirit will help me." "My best friend wants me to come over to watch R-rated movies. Pray that I can fight the temptation.")

3. Talk with your pastor and/or your congregation's worship leaders about an appropriate song the children of the congregation could sing to close each baptismal service (e.g., "Go, My Children, with My Blessing"). Practice it with the children until they can sing it with enthusiasm. If you use the same song each time, and if the words tell about the wonderful blessings God conveys to us through our Baptism, the practice can easily become a meaningful tradition for both the children and the adults in the congregation.

4. Explain to your class the importance of remembering each day who God has made us in Baptism. Then let them help you design some kind of wall hanging each child can display in his or her bedroom to help spark a daily remembrance. The craft need not be elaborate. Check Christian craft books for ideas.

5. Deliberately teach the children how to confess their sins and to remind themselves of Jesus' promise to forgive and empower us. See "A Baptized Sinner" in chapter 5. Explain the process in age-appropriate language and use examples of sins the children will recognize from their own lives. Stress the power God gives through Baptism to repent—to turn around and head toward God rather than continuing on a course away from Him.

6. Encourage progressively deeper study of God's Word as the children in your congregation grow older. Provide Bible story books for the youngest children, children's Bibles for those who have learned to read, and youth Bibles with study notes for the congregation's confirmands. Make sure older teens and adults in the congregation know about helps for personal Bible reading and family devotions. Remember, the Holy Spirit nurtures His baptized people through His Word. But we need to be in that Word in order to receive the strength for growth He promises to provide.

[Jesus said,] "Go and make disciples of all nations, baptizing them in the name of the Father and of the Son and of the Holy Spirit, and teaching them to obey everything I have commanded you. And surely I am with you always, to the very end of the age." (Matthew 28:19–20)

APPENDIX

Baptism in the Early Christian Church

The practice of Baptism in early church history can give us new insights into Baptism. The practice of Baptism predates Christianity. The Scriptures themselves suggest this as they tell of the rite as practiced by John, Christ's forerunner. All four Gospels mention that John baptized Jesus (Matthew 3:13–17; Mark 1:9–11; Luke 3:21–22; John 1:31–34).

JOHN'S BAPTISM

Because of John's identification with Baptism, we call him John the Baptizer or John the Baptist. John defined the rite as he practiced it; He called it a baptism "for repentance" (Matthew 3:11).

Jesus did not need such a baptism, for He had no sin of which to repent. Still, He wanted to be baptized "to fulfill all righteousness," to indicate His consecration to doing His heavenly Father's will. At this baptism, God the Father declared His approval of His Son. Furthermore, Jesus' baptism announced the beginning of His mission on our behalf. With His baptism, Jesus fully identified with us, with our sin and our failures. As we have noted, He Himself did not need cleansing, but even in baptism He became our substitute, as well as our example.

John's baptism was clearly rooted in a rite practiced within Judaism, both before the time of Christ's ministry on earth and after. Male converts to Judaism were required not only to be circumcised, but also to be baptized as an act of repentance. (We might expect that the cleansing function of baptism would in some form, and for various reasons, be practiced in other religions and philosophies, as indeed it was.) So far as Judaism is concerned, the origin of baptism, although uncertain, probably can be traced back to the Levitical washings of the Old Testament.

John the Baptizer's reference to Christ who would "baptize ... with the Holy Spirit and with fire" (Matthew 3:11) predicted the spiritual purification that God would provide through Christ's crucifixion and resurrection. This distinguishes Christian Baptism from John's. John's baptism seems to have been based on human decision to repent. Christian Baptism is God's means of grace through which He gives faith to us, grants us forgiveness of sins and the new life in Jesus Christ.

THE NECESSITY AND BENEFITS OF BAPTISM

The apostle Peter declared Baptism to be the sacrament of admission into the kingdom of God. With Baptism would come salvation and the gift of the Holy Spirit (Acts 2:38). The apostle Paul emphasized that Baptism provided cleansing from sin through a new relationship to Jesus Christ, as well as a participation in His death and resurrection (1 Corinthians 6:11, Galatians 3:26–27, Romans 6:4, Colossians 2:12).

From the beginning, the early Christian church saw Baptism as indispensable. Remember Jesus' words to Nicodemus: "I tell you the truth, no one can enter the kingdom of God unless he is born of water and the spirit" (John 3:5). Also, Mark records the risen Christ as promising, "Whoever believes and is baptized will be saved" (Mark 16:16).

The early church fathers give us a few clues as to their attitude toward, and practice of, Baptism. Hermes, who lived from A.D. 100–140, called Baptism the foundation of the church which "is builded upon waters." By the second century, the church generally agreed that Baptism washed away all previous sins and could be received only once. This view of Baptism limited it, allowing that it provided forgiveness of sins only up to the time of an individual's Baptism. When the New Testament canon was established, the doctrine of Baptism expanded to include the promise of the forgiveness of *all* sins committed throughout life. The written, inspired Word of God made this teaching clear and the church as a whole adopted it.

THE FORMULA OF BAPTISM

On the day of Pentecost, Peter urged his listeners to be baptized "in the name of Jesus Christ" (Acts 2:38; see also Acts 8:16, 10:48, 19:5; Romans 6:3; and Galatians 3:27). The Trinitarian formula (in the name of the Father and of the Son and of the Holy Spirit) employed in Baptism is, of course, drawn from Christ's Great Commission in Matthew 28:19. This baptismal formula was later expanded to become the Apostles' Creed, and this creed—to emphasize its primacy among the creeds—was always used in the baptismal rite, as it is to this day.

The *Didache*, or "Teaching of the Twelve"—a reference to the early disciples—was written about A.D. 100–120, probably in Alexandria, Egypt. The book gives us significant insight into the teachings and practices of the early church. It provides us the fullest early evidence about the method of Baptism:

> *Baptize in the name of the Father and of the Son and of the Holy Spirit in living [running] water. But if thou hast not living water, then baptize in other water; and if thou art not able in cold, then in warm. But if thou hast neither, then pour water upon the head thrice in the name of the Father and of the Son and of the Holy Spirit.*

INFANT BAPTISM

The first reference to infant Baptism in early church literature is by Irenaeus, about A.D. 185. The idea that Baptism washed away only sins committed previous to Baptism encouraged some to delay receiving the Sacrament as long as possible. Constantine waited for his Baptism until his death bed. And Tertullian doubted whether it was wise to baptize the unmarried! But Origin considered infant Baptism to have been practiced by the apostles themselves. And Cyprian, because of concern that being unbaptized would condemn a person, favored Baptism as early as possible.

Infant Baptism can also be supported from an implicit understanding that the words "all nations" in the Great Commission include children. Then too we have the record of the jailer of Philippi being baptized, "he and all his family" (Acts 16:33). As we go back to Pentecost, we hear Peter say that "the promise [of for- giveness and of the gift of the Holy Spirit] is for you *and your children*" (Acts 2:39, emphasis added). Even so, it seems that infant Baptism was not practiced universally throughout the church until the sixth century.

EARLY BAPTISMAL RITUALS

Immersion probably was the most commonly practiced form of Baptism in the early church, as is evident from the *Didache* passage quoted above. The imagery of Romans 6:4 and Colossians 2:12 might have influenced the widespread acceptance of Baptism by immersion. Immersion continues to be the prevailing practice in the Eastern Church to this day, including the immersion of babies. But it should be underscored that according to the *Didache*, pouring baptismal water was also permitted in the early church.

Gradually, more elaborate Baptism rituals developed. By the time of Tertullian, the ceremony included a formal renunciation of the devil and his works by the candidate, then a threefold immersion. Leaving the font, the newly baptized person tasted a mixture of milk and honey to symbolize his or her condition as a newborn babe in Christ (1 Peter 2:2–3). This was followed by an anointing with oil. Then the officiant would lay on hands on the baptized person as token of the bestowal of the Holy Spirit (Acts 8:18, 2 Timothy 1:6, Hebrews 6:1–2). This seems to indicate that in very early church history, Baptism and what we know today as confirmation were combined. Tertullian also reports the use of baptismal sponsors.

PRACTICES AND PREPARATION

Baptism in the early church seems to have been administered not only by the apostles and other leaders, but also by exemplary members in the church. Tertullian noted Baptism's administration in these words:

> *"Of giving it, the chief priest, who is the bishop, has the right; in the next place the presbyters and deacons ... besides these even laymen have the right, for what is equally received can be equally given."*

This seems to have contributed to our present practice that allows any Christian to baptize in an emergency.

Converts to Christianity in the early church were frequently baptized on Easter Sunday or on Pentecost. They prepared for Baptism by fasting, prayer, night-long vigils, and the confession of sins. Catechetical instruction preceded the Baptism. This instruction could last as long as three years. Catechumens preparing for Baptism were permitted to attend the first part of the worship service, but were required to leave before the Lord's Supper, since they had not yet finished their instruction and were not yet baptized.

WHAT WAS BAPTISM IN THE EARLY CHURCH LIKE?

Though the record is sketchy, by adding some reasonable details, picture the practice and significance of Baptism for those early Christians. Doing so can help us more fully appreciate Baptism's significance for us today. Here then, is one possible scenario, a composite of the rituals that developed as the early church baptized new members into the body of Christ:

> *Outside it is dark. It is Easter Eve. The Easter Vigil has been kept, commemorating the hours that Christ has laid in the grave. A group of about 20 to 30 people, with children and babes in arms also present, have gathered around a spiritual leader. In the place where*

they have kept the Easter Vigil, a stream of water rushes into a pool. With the Easter Vigil, they have dramatized and felt the deep meaning of Christ's death for them. Now, anticipating His resurrection, they want to experience His rising from the grave. Baptized in the water, they will come out of it to a new life.

The adults among them have completed weeks, and in some cases, months of instruction. The children too who can comprehend, have received instruction. Parents, concerned that their smallest children should not be deprived of membership in the kingdom of God, have been assured in their instruction that the promise of forgiveness and the gift of the Holy Spirit is also for their children. Faith is a gift of God. And if it is God's gift, then surely children too can receive it. Parents have agreed to speak on behalf of their infants; to promise also that in teaching their children the truths of Scripture and in bringing them to worship, the children will in time, be able in time to express the faith God gives them. Sponsors, or godparents, also stand by, to promise their help in the children's Christian rearing. It is still a time of persecution for Christians, and should parents be martyred, godparents would take on the responsibility of rearing the children in the Christian faith.

All to be baptized are asked their names. Parents supply the names of the children unable to respond for themselves. The sign of the cross is made on each forehead and over each heart. Each candidate tastes salt to symbolize the purification to take place in Baptism. An exorcism of Satan follows. Scripture lessons are then read. Prayers are prayed, followed by the Lord's Prayer. The Creed is recited.

The group now steps forward, closer to the water. The adults and the children who can talk, "renounce the devil and all his works and all his ways"—a phrase still used in our Baptism service today. Parents and godparents again speak on behalf of the infants. Each person is anointed with oil as the cross is signed on the breast and between the shoulder blades. Then follows an admonition to the sponsors on behalf of the infant children present.

The group steps down into the water. The officiant immerses each adult three times, reciting the Trinitarian formula. Those infirm and all infants, probably have water poured over their heads, again three times, as the Trinitarian form is recited.

Those being baptized enter the water without clothing, to symbolize that nothing must get between them and Christ. (As stated in chapter 4, men and women were baptized separately. Deaconesses baptized the women while the pastor or bishop stood behind a screen and spoke the words.) Then, as they step out of the water, they put on white robes, symbolic of Jesus' righteousness covering them wholly.

Lighted candles are given to them. The officiant speaks the words of Christ reminding them that now, reborn, they are to be light in the world. They are to reflect Christ, the Light, so that their good works, seen by all, will bring praise to the heavenly Father (Matthew 5:16).

Now the baptized are ushered into another room where the adults and the older children among them will partake of the Eucharist. They have been received into the body of Christ and now for the first time come to the Holy Table where they will receive Christ's forgiveness again and again throughout earthly life.

We cannot, of course, insist that this picture of Baptism in the early church is accurate in each detail. It serves as a composite of the rituals that developed in the practice of Baptism.

CONDITIONS FOR CREDIT

1. No fewer than six 60-minute class sessions shall be held.
2. Attendance at 75% of the class sessions shall be required.
3. At least one hour of preparation shall be requested of all students in advance of each of the class sessions.
4. The textbooks and instructor's guides recommended by the Department of Child Ministry of the Lutheran Church—Missouri Synod shall be used.
5. An instructor other than the pastor ought to be approved by the local pastor in order to obtain credit for students. This approval shall be indicated by the pastor's signature on the application blank for credit.
6. The application for credit should be sent to the Department of Child Ministry immediately after the completion of the course.

APPLICATION FOR CREDIT

To be sent to Department of Child Ministry
1333 S. Kirkwood Rd., St. Louis, Mo 63122-7295

Name of congregation: _____

Address of congregation: _____
(Street and number or R.F.D.)

_____
(City)   (State)   (Zip)

Name of course for which credit is desired: _____

Dates on which lessons were conducted: _____

_____

Length of class sessions in minutes:_____Number registered in
class_____

The persons on the following list have met all the requirements in regard to attendance, preparation for class work, and final test and are recommended to receive credit.

(Signed)_____Instructor

Date:_____
(Signed)_____Pastor

If the instructor of the course is not the pastor of the congregation, there should be two signatures: the instuctor's and the pastor's.

(Pleases type or print)   **Last Name**   **First Name**
Middle

1._____

2._____

3._____

4._____

5._____

6._____

7._____

8._____

9._____